THE
STEAM
LOCOMOTIVE
SHED

· BRITAIN'S LIFE AND TIMES ·

THE STEAM LOCOMOTIVE SHED

A *further illustrated tribute*

Roger Siviter ARPS

· RAILWAY HERITAGE ·

from

The NOSTALGIA Collection

First published in 2001

British Library Cataloguing in Publication Data

A catalogue record for this book is available from the British Library.

ISBN 1 85794 108 X

Silver Link Publishing Ltd
The Trundle
Ringstead Road
Great Addington
Kettering
Northants
NN14 4BW

Tel/Fax: 01536 330588
email: sales@nostalgiacollection.com
Website: www.nostalgiacollection.com

Printed and bound in Great Britain

A Silver Link book
from
The NOSTALGIA Collection

Frontispiece Sunset at Croes Newydd shed (Wrexham) on Monday 13 March 1967, as BR Standard Class 4 2-6-0 No 76088 prepares to leave the shed yard. This shed, when in the Western Region, was numbered 84J, but with boundary changes in the early 1960s to the London Midland Region it became 6C. It closed on 5 June of that year.

ACKNOWLEDGEMENTS

In compiling this book I have many people to thank, including Hugh Ballantyne, my wife Christina, Silver Link Publishing Ltd and, most of all, not only the drivers and firemen, but the men who ran and worked at the locomotive shed, without whom none of this would have been possible.
    Except where otherwise credited, all pictures were taken by the author.

CONTENTS

DO NOT CLIMB ABOVE FOOTPLATE LEVEL WHEN UNDER ELECTRIFIED WIRES

BATH GREEN PARK M.P. Depot   BRITISH RAILWAYS   WESTERN Region   B.R. 32710/3

1 WEEK   ENGINEMEN'S ROSTERS   Commencing   28·2·1966

Driver	Firemen	SUNDAY On Duty	SUNDAY Turn/Dia. No.	MONDAY On Duty	MONDAY Turn/Dia. No.	TUESDAY On Duty	TUESDAY Turn/Dia. No.	WEDNESDAY On Duty	WEDNESDAY Turn/Dia. No.	THURSDAY On Duty	THURSDAY Turn/Dia. No.	FRIDAY On Duty	FRIDAY Turn/Dia. No.	SATURDAY On Duty	SATURDAY Turn/Dia. No.
N. GIBBONS				6·45	Pass	6·45	Pass	6·45	Pass	6·45	Pass	6·45	Pass	REST	DAY
	M. RYALL			"	"	"	"	"	"	"	"	"	"	REST	DAY
	T. DAVIS			2	12/30 K	REST	DAY	2	12/30 K	2	1/30 K	REST	DAY	2	12/30 K
	E. WEBBER			2	2/45 R	2	2/45 R	2	2/45 R	REST	DAY	2	2/45 R	2	2/45 R
C. WALDRON				4/25	Pass	4/25	Pass	4/25	Pass	REST	DAY	4/25	Pass	4/25	Pass
	E. PAULLEY			2	4/30 K	2	4/30 K	2	4/30 K	REST	DAY	2	4/30 K	2	4/30 K
A. GUNNING				8·15	Pass	8·15	Pass	REST	DAY	8·15	Pass	8·15	Pass	8·15	Pass
	D. MASSEY			4/0	R.F.	4/0	R.F.	REST	DAY	4/0	R.F.	4/0	R.F.	12/0	R.F.
W. GUNNING				6·20	Goods		Spare	8·15	Pass		Spare	REST	DAY	6·30	Relief
A. WILLIAMS				L	R	L	R	4/0	R.F.	L	R	L	R	REST	DAY
	J. BURROUGHS			L	EAVE	11·55	Goods	11·55	Goods	Per	11·5 Bus	2	7·0 L	REST	DAY
F. BEARD				L	R	L	R	L	R	L	R	L	R	REST	DAY
J. STAMP					SPARE	12/30	Relief	REST	DAY	4/25	Pass	2/45	Relief	3/25	Goods
	I. BUNNETT				SPARE	12/30	Relief	REST	DAY	4/25	Pass	2/45	Relief	3/25	Goods
D. HOLDEN				12·0	R.F.	6·20	Goods	6·20	Goods	REST	DAY	6·20	Goods	6·45	Pass
	D. COLES			6·20	Goods	6·20	Goods	6·20	Goods	REST	DAY	6·20	Goods	6·45	Pass
S. CATER				L	R	L	R	L	R	L	R	L	R	REST	DAY
	T. COX			4/30	Relief	4/30	Relief	4/30	Relief	REST	DAY	4/30	Relief	4/30	Relief
	A. PARSONS			5·25	Shunt	L	EAVE	L	EAVE	L	EAVE		Spare	REST	DAY
C. HAMILTON				9/25	Goods	9/25	Goods	9/25	Goods	9/25	Goods	REST	DAY		SPARE
	G. HUGGINS			"	"	"	"	"	"	"	"	REST	DAY	"	"
B. FORD				REST	DAY	4·40	Goods	4·40	Goods	4·40	Goods	4·40	Goods	4·40	Goods
	J. SAWYER			REST	DAY	"	"	"	"	"	"	"	"	"	"
H. STARKEY				SICK		SICK		SICK		SICK		SICK		REST	DAY
F. HEMMINGS				11·55	Goods	REST	DAY	11·55	Goods	11·55	Goods	11·55	Goods		SPARE
	C. FELL			"	"	REST	DAY		SPARE	"	"	"	"		SPARE
R. ADAMS				7·0	Loco	11·55	Goods		SPARE	6·20	Goods	REST	DAY	3·15	Goods
	D. PILLINGER			7·0	Loco		SPARE		SPARE	6·20	Goods	REST	DAY	3·15	Goods
R. BEESLEY				4·0	SPARE		SPARE		SPARE	REST	DAY		SPARE		SPARE
	J. PITT			REST	DAY	5·25	Shunt	5·25	Shunt	5·25	Shunt	5·25	Shunt	5·25	Shunt
W. RAWLES				SICK		SICK		SICK		SICK		REST	DAY	SICK	
	B. REYNOLDS			2/45	Relief	2/45	Relief	2/45	Relief	2/45	Relief	REST	DAY	2/45	Relief
G. TUCKER				3·0	Spare	3·15	Goods	3·15	Goods	3·15	Goods	3·15	Goods	REST	DAY
	D. NORMAN			3·0	Spare	3·15	Goods	3·15	Goods	3·15	Goods	3·15	Goods	REST	DAY
R. WILLIAMS				6·0	SPARE		SPARE	REST	DAY	4/30	Relief	9/25	Goods		SPARE
	L. HANKS			6·0	SPARE		SPARE	REST	DAY	4/30	Relief	9/25	Goods		SPARE
D. LEVI				REST	DAY	3·0	Spare		SPARE		Spare		Spare		SPARE
	C. HOLDER			REST	DAY										
K. NORRIS				12/10	Shunt	12/10	Shunt	12/10	Shunt	12/10	Shunt	12/10	Shunt	REST	DAY
	R. GILLUM			1/0	Goods	1/0	Goods	1/0	Goods	1/0	Goods	1/0	Goods	REST	DAY
W. HUNT				1/0	Goods	1/0	Goods	1/0	Goods	1/0	Goods	1/0	Goods	REST	DAY
	T. HUGHES			Per	11·5 Bus	Per	11·5 Bus	Per	11·5 Bus	8·15	Pass	Per	11·5 Bus	REST	DAY
D. LATHAM				5·25	Shunt	7·0	Loco	7·0	Loco	7·0	Loco	REST	DAY	7·0	Loco
	A. LARCOMBE			8·15	Pass	8·15	Pass	8·15	Pass	REST	DAY	8·15	Pass	8·15	Pass
T. GUNNING				L	R	L	R	L	R	L	R	L	R	REST	DAY
	S. SHELLARD			12/10	Shunt	12/10	Shunt	12/10	Shunt	12/10	Shunt	12/10	Shunt	REST	DAY
	W. MAYO			4/25	Pass	4/25	Pass	4/25	Pass	REST	DAY	4/25	Pass	4/25	Pass
W. H. SHEARN				REST	DAY	5·25	Shunt	5·25	Shunt	5·25	Shunt	5·25	Shunt	5·25	Shunt
	H. C. REYNOLDS			REST	DAY	7·0	Loco	7·0	Loco	7·0	Loco	7·0	Loco	7·0	Loco
	A. K. BROWN			12/30	Relief	REST	DAY	12/30	Relief	12/30	Relief	12/30	Relief	12/30	Relief
E. HEMMINGS				6·30	Relief	6·30	Relief	6·30	Relief	6·30	Relief	6·30	Relief	REST	DAY
	P. EVANS													REST	DAY

DRIVERS AND FIREMEN MUST EXAMINE THE ALTERATION SHEET DAILY

INTRODUCTION

During my 'loco spotting' days in the late 1940s and early 1950s, I only visited a handful of sheds. The ones that I remember most of all are Tyseley shed on a sunny summer evening in 1949, with the shed yard (situated by Warwick Road) crammed full of GWR locomotives, and Aberystwyth shed in August 1951. The latter was situated at the end of the platform (between the Machynlleth and Carmarthen lines) and contained several GWR 'Dukedog' 9400 Class 4-4-0s and 'Manor' Class 4-6-0s. I suppose the reason I went to only a few sheds was because there was so much to see on the main line and at large stations such as Birmingham Snow Hill and New Street, and also because it was not easy for a schoolboy to get round sheds without being in an organised party.

So when I started photographing at the end of 1965, I was determined to visit and photograph as many sheds as I could, not only to make up for past lost opportunities, but also to feel and capture the atmosphere that is unique to a locomotive shed and its environment. For even in the last few years of steam there were some terrific sheds to visit. I have also been fortunate enough to be able to include some 1950s shed scenes taken by my good friend Hugh Ballantyne, which has added considerably to the balance of the book.

The book is divided into nine sections, the titles of which I think are self-explanatory, and cover the day-to-day scene as it was at a locomotive shed. Included in the sections are industrial locomotive sheds, which was so much a part of our industrial heritage, while the final section, 'The new age', shows sheds that have been converted or rebuilt for use by today's traction.

Roger Siviter
Evesham

Left Dated 28 February 1966, this is the very last weekly roster sheet posted at Bath Green Park shed and shows the names of all the Bath drivers and firemen at the close of the Somerset & Dorset (S&D) line. *Hugh Ballantyne*

THE STEAM LOCOMOTIVE SHED

1.
INSIDE VIEW

Left The former Southern Railway shed at Salisbury (70E) plays host to 'Battle of Britain' 'Pacific' No 34060 *25 Squadron* and 'West Country' 'Pacific' No 34098 *Templecombe* on the last day of Southern steam, 2 July 1967. *Hugh Ballantyne*

Below left Steam working lasted in the Isle of Wight until the end of 1966 and, on 21 July of that year, Class 02 0-4-4 tank locomotive No 17 *Seaview* is seen in the shed at St Johns (Ryde) alongside No 14 *Fishbourne*. These delightful tank engines were designed by Adams for the

LSWR and introduced in 1889. One example, No 24 *Calbourne*, has been preserved by the Wight Locomotive Society at Havenstreet on the IOW Steam Railway.

Below Salisbury was always noted for the cleanliness of its locomotives, as illustrated by this view of BR Standard Class 4 2-6-4 tank locomotive No 80152 inside the shed on the morning of 7 April 1966. Behind is BR Standard Class 4 2-6-0 No 76007. Both these engines were withdrawn from service in July 1967, the 2-6-0 having been built in 1953 and the 2-6-4T in 1957.

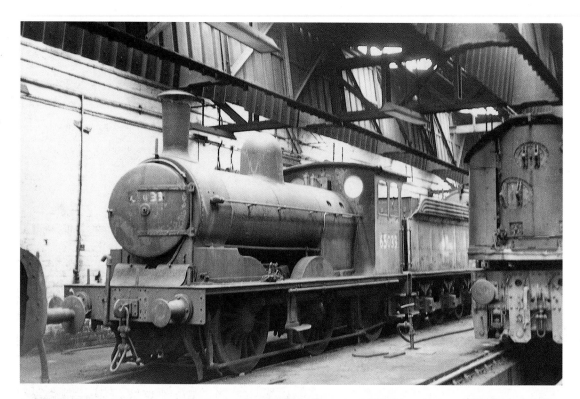

THE STEAM LOCOMOTIVE SHED

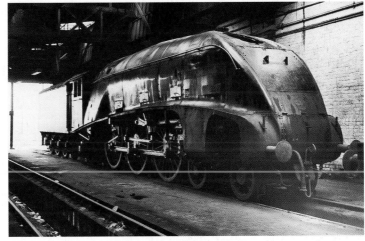

Above left We leave the South of England and travel to the North East where, on 1 April 1966, Darlington shed was home to Class J21 0-6-0 No 65033, introduced by Worsdell in 1886 for the North Eastern Railway. This locomotive had been withdrawn some years earlier and was destined for preservation at the North of England Open Air Museum at Beamish.

Left Now the home of the National Railway Museum, on Sunday 1 May 1966 York shed (50A) was still home to many LNER locomotives, including this Class K1 2-6-0 No 62046, seen beside Class B1 4-6-0 No 61019. Unlike Darlington, which was a straight shed, York was a roundhouse with tracks radiating from a central turntable. Also inside the shed on that day, according to my records, were Class V2 2-6-2s Nos 60824 and 608319, B1s Nos 61035 and 61238, BR Standard Class 3 2-6-0 No 77012, BR Standard Class 9F 2-10-0 No 92137, and ex-LMS Class 4MT 2-6-0 No 43071.

Top Sunshine and shadows abound in this picture taken at North Blythe shed (52F) on 1 June 1966. The Class J27 0-6-0 locomotives clustered round the turntable are No 65869 and, straight ahead, Nos 65880 and 65801 together with an unidentified member of the class. These former North Eastern locomotives worked in the North East until September 1967 when they were withdrawn. One example of the class,

No 2392 (65894), is preserved and works on the North Yorkshire Moors Railway. *Hugh Ballantyne*

Above This North Eastern quartet is completed by another picture taken at Darlington shed on 1 April 1966, this time of ex-LNER A4 'Pacific' No 60010 *Dominion of Canada*, which was in store pending preservation in Canada at the Montreal Railway Historical Museum. Darlington shed (51A) had closed a few days before these pictures were taken. Also in store in the shed were the last two LNER A1 Class 'Pacifics', Nos 60124 *Kenilworth* and 60145 *Saint Mungo*. I saw No 60145 in York shed yard on 1 May (see pages 65), from where it ran a few more trips before withdrawal a few weeks later on 19 June.

THE STEAM LOCOMOTIVE SHED

These three views are what might be termed 'inside, looking out', as was often the case when taking shed pictures.

The first was taken on the 15-inch-gauge Romney, Hythe & Dymchurch Railway at New Romney shed on 16 August 1969, and shows 4-6-2 No 8 *Hurricane* receiving attention outside the shed building. On the extreme right is the tender of No 7 *Typhoon*, another beautiful 'Pacific' locomotive. Note also the turntable on the left.

The second photograph shows ex-LMS 'Jubilee' Class 4-6-0 No 45581 *Bihar and Orissa* staring out of Farnley Junction shed (55C) at the wintry conditions of 2 April 1966.

The trio is completed by a scene taken in Salisbury shed a few days later on 7 April, showing 'Battle of Britain' Class 'Pacific' No 34089 *602 Squadron* and BR Standard Class 4 4-6-0 No 75068. It is nice to see the 'Battle of Britain' still with its nameplate, for by this time many had been removed.

Many Great Western sheds were roundhouses, and this next picture, taken at St Philips Marsh shed (82B) in Bristol on 3 June 1963 well illustrates this. On the extreme left is shadowy ex-GWR 'Hall' Class 4-6-0 No 5974 *Wallsworth Hall*, while the rest of the picture features, from left to right, 'Castle' Class 4-6-0 No 5050 *Earl of St Germans*, Class 4700 2-8-0 No 4701 and 'County' Class 4-6-0 No 1020 *County of Monmouth*. What a mouth-watering line-up of GWR locomotives! *Hugh Ballantyne*

THE STEAM LOCOMOTIVE SHED

Another lovely sight, this time at Swindon shed (82C) on 11 September 1955, featuring one of the classic 'Star' locomotives, No 4062 *Malmesbury Abbey*. This class was designed by Churchward and introduced in 1906. No 4062 was one of the last survivors, being withdrawn in November 1956. I well remember seeing several of these magnificent four-cylinder locomotives at Snow Hill station in my spotting days in Birmingham in the late 1940s, including (according to my reference book) Nos 4007, 4013, 4018, 4021, 4023, 4026, 4028, 4031, 4033, 4049, 4051, 4052, 4053, 4058, 4060 and finally No 4062. Happy days! *Hugh Ballantyne*

THE STEAM LOCOMOTIVE SHED

Left Carnforth shed (10A) was one of the final steam sheds on BR, and after August 1968 became known as 'Steamtown Carnforth', playing host to the many preserved steam locomotives that worked in the North West, as indeed it still does today. With only a few months to go before the end of BR steam, ex-LMS Class 5 4-6-0 No 45342 simmers away inside the shed on 16 April 1968. Note the '10A' shedplate on the smokebox door and the shed name on the buffer beam. It is also worth mentioning that the shed (in LMS and early BR days) was numbered 11A, followed by 24L, and finally 10A.

Above The shed at Tebay was mainly used to house the Shap banking engines. It was originally a sub-shed of Carnforth and numbered 11E, but was later renumbered 12E and came under 12A Carlisle Kingmoor. On 30 March 1966 ex-LMS Fairburn Class 4MT 2-6-4 tank No 42210 shines like a black cherry in the gloom of the shed. Behind is another Fairburn 2-6-4 tank, No 42232, and on the right is Ivatt Class 4MT 2-6-0 No 43033.

Right On 24 April 1966 Chester shed (6A) plays host to ex-LMS Hughes/ Fowler Class 5MT 2-6-0 No 42765. These 'Moguls', popularly known as 'Crabs', were first introduced in 1926 and ended their days in the Chester area. Happily three examples of the class are preserved, including No 42765.

Above Ex-WD 2-8-0 No 90722 and Ivatt Class 4MT 2-6-0 No 43125 find themselves side by side at Normanton shed (55E) on the morning of Sunday 3 April 1966. As can be seen, the shed was crammed with engines, including 'Black Five' 4-6-0s, WD 2-8-0s, LMS 8F 2-8-0s and Fairburn 2-6-4 tanks. The strange effect above No 43125 is caused by a spray of water from a locomotive piercing the shafts of sunlight coming through the shed roof.

Below Another West Riding shed, Stourton (55B), was visited on the afternoon of 2 April 1966, and contained among the 8Fs and others a few examples of BR Standard Class 3MT 2-6-0s, one of which was the first of the class, No 77000, seen here inside the shed building. Only 20 of this class were built, and they had a short life; introduced in 1954, by July 1967 they had all been withdrawn. Unlike the Standard Class 2MT 2-6-0s, none survived into preservation.

THE STEAM LOCOMOTIVE SHED

Above In BR days the former GWR Banbury shed was originally a Western Region facility (84C), but with boundary changes it came under the London Midland Region and was renumbered 2D. Consequently, by the beginning of 1966, instead of 'Halls' and 'Granges', it had an allocation of ex- LMS 'Black Fives' and 8Fs, as well as BR Standard Classes, mainly 9F 2-10-0s for use on the iron ore trains from the quarries of Northamptonshire to the West Midlands. On 26 February 1966 4-6-0 No 44865 is seen inside the shed nose-to-nose with another unidentified 'Black Five'.

Right The delightful little shed at Cromford was situated by the canal at the foot of the first rope incline on the Cromford & High Peak line, some three-quarters of a mile from the junction of the High Peak line and the Derby-Matlock line. It was used to house the engine that shunted the sidings by the canal wharf. On 17 May 1966 ex-LMS Class 0F 0-4-0 saddle tank No 47006, designed by Kitson in 1932 to Stanier's requirements, sits in the shed after its day's work is done. The Cromford & High Peak line sadly closed on 30 April 1967, but the trackbed is now used as a footpath and cycle route, and there is a visitor centre at Middleton Top.

Sunshine and shadows highlight men and machines at Croes Newydd shed, Wrexham, on 13 March 1967.

THE STEAM LOCOMOTIVE SHED

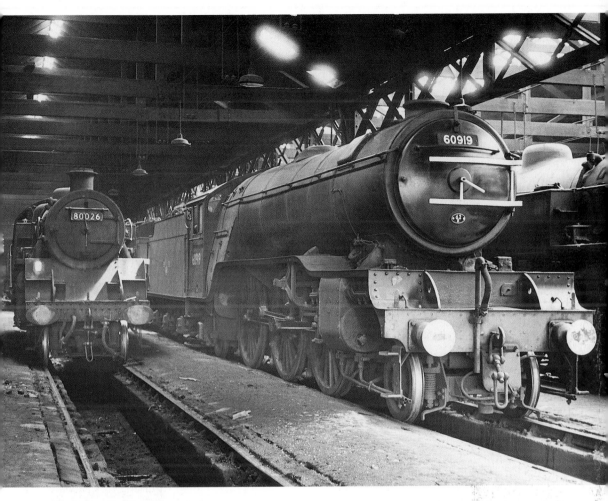

St Margarets shed (64A) was situated about 1½ miles east of Edinburgh Waverley station. It was the principal freight shed in the Edinburgh area, and at one time had an allocation of over 220 locomotives. By the time this picture was taken, on Sunday 19 June 1966, I counted about a dozen locomotives on or around the shed, including this nicely turned-out ex-LNER Class V2 2-6-2 No 60919 with a 62B Dundee shedplate. On the left is Standard Class 4MT 2-6-4 tank No 80026, and just visible on the right is 2-6-4 tank No 80055. At the back of the shed and not really photographable was the last ex-LNER A3 Class 'Pacific' (except *Flying Scotsman*) No 60041 *Salmon Trout*. The depot closed in April 1967.

Overleaf These three pictures I hope show the effect that sunshine, shadows and smoke created inside an engine shed. The first was taken at Stourton shed on 2 April 1966 and shows, from left to right, Class 3MT 2-6-0 No 77003, Class 5MT 4-6-0 No 45079 and another Class 3MT 2-6-0, this time No 77013. The next scene shows Standard Class 4MT 2-6-4 tank No 80089 at Nine Elms shed (70A) in South London on 29 May 1966. Finally, on 25 April 1968 at Heaton Mersey shed (9F) Standard Class 9F 2-10-0 No 92069 is seen facing 'Black Five' No 45190.

THE STEAM LOCOMOTIVE SHED

Top The former Midland Railway shed at Burton-on-Trent (17B) is the setting for ex-LMS Class 8F 2-8-0 No 48700 as it languishes in one of its two spacious roundhouses on the afternoon of Saturday 30 April 1966. Note the arched entrances to the adjacent roundhouse.

Above On the afternoon of Sunday 1 May 1966 BR Standard Class 3MT 2-6-0 No 77012 is seen in the vast roundhouse of York shed. Note the shed code on the locomotive – 50D (Goole).

THE STEAM LOCOMOTIVE SHED

BR Standard Class 4MT 4-6-0 No 75002 rests between duties in Croes Newydd roundhouse
on the afternoon of 13 March 1967.

INSIDE VIEW

Above A very smoky scene at Stoke shed (5D) on the evening of 24 April 1966. Clustered around the turntable are a Class 08 diesel shunter, ex-LMS Ivatt Class 4MT 2-6-0 No 43115 and ex-Midland Railway Class 3F 0-6-0 tank No 47273. The latter tank engines were known as 'Jinties', and the 4MT 2-6-0s as 'Pigs'. Happily, both classes have survived into preservation. I don't know how long the shed roof had been missing, but the recesses where the roof-beams had been secured can be plainly seen.

Below Westhouses shed (18B) was situated a few miles south of Clay Cross junction on the Midland Railway line to Toton and Trent Junction, and provided motive power for the many coal and goods trains that served this industrial area of the East Midlands. And so, on 17 May 1966, it was no surprise to see a pair of ex-LMS 8F 2-8-0s, Nos 48214 and 48159, simmering away inside the shed building. Note the pile of firebars. Also on shed that day, but not in use, were a pair of Midland Railway Class 4F 0-6-0s Nos 44203 and 44218; the latter was fitted with a tender cab for working in the Peak District.

We finish the 'Inside view' section with this picture of two ex-GWR 0-6-0 Class 5700 pannier tanks, Nos 3607 and 9608, as they 'snooze away' inside Stourbridge roundhouse on Sunday 3 July 1966. The shed closed to steam on the 11th, shortly after this picture was taken, but I believe that it was used to stable diesel locomotives until finally closing by the end of 1966. Stourbridge was originally a GWR shed, coded 84F, but with boundary changes was renumbered 2C in the early 1960s. However, as can be seen, right until the end it was still home to a few ex-GWR locomotives.

2.
OUTSIDE VIEW

Left I thought it was always exciting when you walked down the path to the shed, turned the corner to the front and were confronted by a sight like this Hughes/Fowler 'Crab' 2-6-0 No 42727. The location is Crewe South (5B), known as Gresty Lane shed, and the date of this sunny spring evening is Sunday 24 April 1966.

Left As if not to be outdone by Crewe South, Heaton Mersey shed (near Stockport) provides a fairly clean 8F 2-8-0, No 48252, to pose in front of the shed building on 25 April 1968, within weeks of the end of BR steam.

Right Lostock Hall shed (10D) at Preston is the setting on a sunny 25 February 1968, as Class 5MT No 45345 prepares to move off the shed, be turned, then run into Preston station to take out the 1752 from Preston to Liverpool. On the right is 8F 2-8-0 No 48253.

THE STEAM LOCOMOTIVE SHED

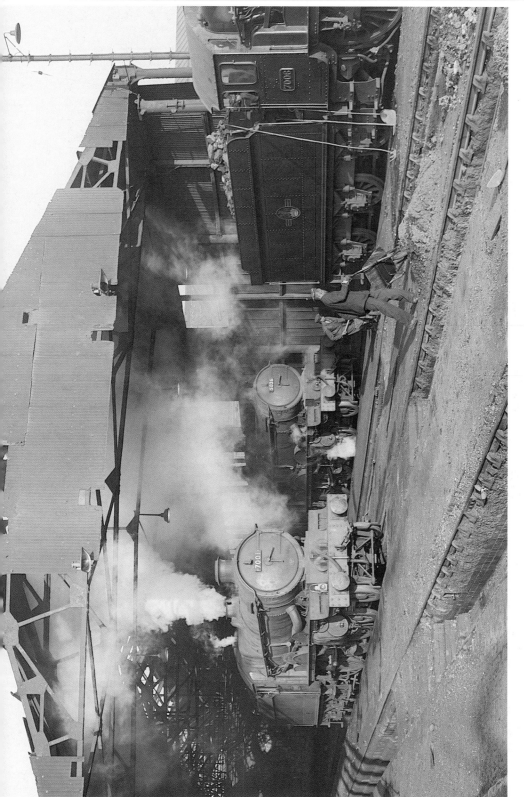

It is early morning at Wolverhampton Stafford Road shed (84A) on 24 August 1963, and ex-GWR 'Castle' Class locomotives Nos 7001 *Sir James Milne*, 5026 *Criccieth Castle* and 7006 *Lydford Castle* are all being prepared to work summer-Saturday trains to holiday destinations in the South West. There was also a locomotive works on this site, which closed in 1964. The locomotive shed itself closed in September 1963, a few weeks after this picture was taken. Until September 1962, when they were withdrawn from service, as many as 11 of the mighty 'King' Class locomotives were shedded at Stafford Road for working the principal Paddington trains, especially from 1960, when there was an hourly service to London. Although the shed looks run-down, right until the end it had a reputation for fine running, a credit to the crews and shed staff. *Hugh Ballantyne*

THE STEAM LOCOMOTIVE SHED

On 9 May 1964 one of Stanier's magnificent 'Coronation' Class 'Pacifics', No 46251 *City of Nottingham*, poses on Swindon shed after working in with a special train from Nottingham, which it would later take back. Beside the 4-6-2 are 'Modified Hall' Class 4-6-0 No 7927 *Willington Hall*, having its smokebox inspected, and 'Castle' Class 4-6-0 No 7022 *Hereford Castle*. The 'Castle' was a standby locomotive for a Western Region/Ian Allan Paddington-Plymouth-Bristol-Paddington high-speed special. *Hugh Ballantyne*

This was the scene at the north end of Doncaster shed (36A) on 2 May 1965, with Class K1 2-6-0 No 62056, with Class 8F 2-8-0 No 90279, Class O4 2-8-0 No 63818, and the tender of BR Standard Class 9F 2-10-0 No 92120. On the left are the shed offices, including that of 'the Gaffer'. *Hugh Ballantyne*

THE STEAM LOCOMOTIVE SHED

Above Ex-LNER Class A2 'Pacific' No 60530 *Sayajirao* is on standby duty at Dundee shed on the morning of 22 June 1966. During the two weeks that I spent in Scotland at this time, although I saw sister engine No 60532 *Blue Peter* several times at work on the main line, my only sight of No 60530 was in and around Tay Bridge shed, Dundee. The locomotive was withdrawn from service the following November.

Below Early in 1966 the former LNER shed at Colwick (40E) had passed into the control of the London Midland Region, and the former LNER locomotives, mainly Class B1 4-6-0s and Class O4 2-8-0s, were quickly being replaced by ex-LMS 'Black Five' 4-6-0s and 8F 2-8-0s. A visit to the shed on Sunday 20 March 1966 shows the change in full swing, with a lone B1, No 61089, surrounded by 8F 2-8-0s.

Above On Sunday 19 June 1966 Class 5MT 4-6-0 No 45477 poses by the side of the main shed at Edinburgh St Margarets. In the background is 4-6-0 No 44791 and an English Electric Type 4 (later Class 40) diesel-electric locomotive. Note the shed name on No 45477's buffer beam – Dalry Road (64C) – which had been the main shed for the Caledonian Railway in Edinburgh, situated to the west of Princes Street station. The typical Edinburgh houses or tenements that characterise this scene are situated on Restalrig Road.

Left Another Scottish shed, this time Perth (63A). In a typical shed scene, ex-LMS 4-6-0 No 44704 sits outside its home shed on the evening of Saturday 18 June 1966. Facing it is the rear of a breakdown crane.

Right By the beginning of July 1968 Bolton shed (9K) had ceased to operate any steam workings. However, a visit to the shed a few weeks earlier on 6 June 1968 showed that there were quite a few locomotives still in steam, including 8F 2-8-0s Nos 48337 and 48773, as well as 'Black Five' 4-6-0s Nos 44947, 45073, 45290 and 45318, shown here outside the shed. Note the very ornate yard lamp.

THE STEAM LOCOMOTIVE SHED

Above There is plenty of pre-Grouping motive power on display at Gillingham (Kent) shed (73D) on 15 March 1959. From the left is former SECR C Class 0-6-0 No 31693, designed by Wainwright, Maunsell D1 Class 4-4-0 No 31509, and another Wainwright design for the SECR, Class H 0-4-4 tank No 31522. *Hugh Ballantyne*

Below More modern motive power is seen at Ramsgate shed (74B) on the same day, including two of the famous ex-SR 'Schools' Class 4-4-0s Nos 30919 *Harrow* and 30921 *Shrewsbury*. Also on display at this surprisingly untidy looking shed are 'West Country' Class 'Pacifics' No 34037 *Clovelly* and the first of the class, No 34001 *Exeter*. *Hugh Ballantyne*

THE STEAM LOCOMOTIVE SHED

This view of the Guildford (70C) half roundhouse was taken on 11 August 1963, and shows 'USA' 0-6-0 tank No 30072 as shed pilot with Class Q1 0-6-0s and Maunsell Class N and U 'Moguls' predominating inside the shed. *Hugh Ballantyne*

These three scenes convey something of the atmosphere of locomotive sheds on murky days, when the smoke and steam combined to give out an ambience that was quite unique. Of course, not recorded here is the tangy sulphurous smell that was also to be experienced.

The first scene shows Banbury shed on the morning of Saturday 26 February 1966, with 'Black Five' 4-6-0s, 8F 2-8-0s and 9F 2-10-0s on show.

A similar scene is enacted at Newton Heath shed (26A) in Manchester on the afternoon of Saturday 18 November 1967, with ex-LMS 8F 2-8-0s Nos 48257, 48026, 48679 and an unidentified member of the same class. Note the fire braziers glowing by the water columns – it was certainly cold that day!

And although it's 17 April 1968 in the third view, it still looks and feels more like a winter's day than springtime as Class 5MT 4-6-0s Nos 45394 and 44963 wait outside Carnforth shed before leaving for their day's work. The intruder on the right is Brush Type 4 diesel (in two-tone livery) No D1572.

I suppose as enthusiasts we look upon scenes like this and think what a wonderful atmosphere, but we would probably think differently if we had to work in conditions like this, surrounded by dirt and coal-dust and often in very cold and wet conditions. Personally, therefore, I have nothing but praise and admiration for the men who worked at these locomotive sheds, as well, of course, as the engine crews.

THE STEAM LOCOMOTIVE SHED

THE STEAM LOCOMOTIVE SHED

Meanwhile, on sunnier days, these next three pictures make interesting comparisons from an architectural point of view. Locomotive sheds seemed to come in all shapes and sizes, depending on needs, etc, and some were far more ornate than others.

The neat-looking former GWR shed in the first view is Severn Tunnel Junction, full of engines on 12 October 1958. From left to right can be seen Class 4MT 2-6-0 tank No 4164, Class 2800 2-8-0 No 3846, 'Hall' Class 4-6-0 No 6903 *Belmont Hall* and another ex-GWR 2-8-0, No 3834.

The second scene shows the former Midland Railway shed at Burton-on-Trent, with ex-LNER K1 Class 2-6-0 No 62012 basking in the sun on the afternoon of Saturday 30 April 1966. The 'Mogul' had worked in from York that morning on an empty beer train. Note the 50A York shed code.

Burton shed was a very attractive-looking building and makes a sharp contrast with the rather utilitarian 'building at Whitland in West Wales, where 0-6-0 pannier tanks Nos 3657 and 8738 (behind) line up by one of the ex-GWR Class 4500 2-6-2 tanks, No 5520. This picture was taken on 9 June 1960. Whitland was in a group of sub-sheds covered by Neyland (87H). *Hugh Ballantyne/ RS/Hugh Ballantyne*

One of the major sheds on the former GWR was at Bristol Bath Road (82A), situated on the east side of the line at the south end of Bristol Temple Meads station. In its heyday as a steam shed, it had a fair-sized allocation of locomotives, including 'Castles', 'Counties', 'Halls' and 'Granges', and at one time was home to 'King' Class 4-6-0 No 6000 *King George V*. This picture, taken on 9 July 1960, gives a good idea of the size of the shed area. The 'Castle' with reporting number 'M96' is No 5078 *Beaufort*, and it is making ready to come off shed to work north on the 10.05 Penzance to Crewe train. The shed was closed to steam on 11 September 1960 and was converted to a diesel depot (see page 126). It must have been wonderful trainspotting here in steam days, with all the action in Temple Meads station together with all the locomotives on the shed. *Hugh Ballantyne*

THE STEAM LOCOMOTIVE SHED

Above Another famous shed (and works) on the former GWR was at Newton Abbot (83A), and, like Bath Road, it was also converted to a diesel depot (see page 103). On 18 May 1958 83A is full of engines including, from left to right, 'Castle' No 4089 *Donnington Castle*, Prairie tank No 5195, 'Castle' No 7000 *Viscount Portal*, Prairie tank No 5108, 'Modified Hall' No 6988 *Swithland Hall*, 2-6-2 tank No 5533 (not visible) and 2-6-2 tanks Nos 5154 and 4145. The shed generally provided the pilot engines for the three fierce banks between Newton Abbot and Plymouth – Dainton, Rattery and Hemerden. Newton Abbot was also the junction station for the line to Paignton, Torquay and Kingswear, so that a summer Saturday in steam days was one long procession of trains, and very well remembered not only by enthusiasts but by the millions of holidaymakers who had travelled to Devon and Cornwall on those steamy 'Summer Saturdays'. *Hugh Ballantyne*

Below Ex-GWR 'Saint' Class 4-6-0 No 2944 *Highnam Court* is seen on Cardiff Canton shed (88A) on 2 September 1951. Alongside is 'Hall' Class 4-6-0 No 4975 *Umberslade Hall*. The 'Hall' Class was derived from the 'Saints', the first 'Hall', No 4900 *Saint Martin*, being a rebuild of 'Saint' No 2925 *Saint Martin*. *Hugh Ballantyne*

Above In nice external condition, ex-Southern Railway 'West Country' 'Pacific' No 34032 *Camelford* is seen outside Salisbury shed on the morning of Thursday 7 April 1966. I have always thought that the rebuilt Southern 'Pacifics' were very handsome engines, and in my opinion this broadside view more than confirms it. No 34032 was rebuilt in 1957 and withdrawn in October 1966. It had the distinction of being in charge of the last normal steam working (as opposed to special trains) to Exeter Central, the 1300 from Waterloo to Exeter on 29 November 1965. It returned on the 1945 'perishables' to Nine Elms.

Below Another broadside view, this time of Fairburn 2-6-4 tank No 42225, used for banking trains up the 5 miles at 1 in 75 of Shap Incline. The location is the modern-looking shed at Tebay and the date is 30 March 1966; No 42225 had been withdrawn by the following June. The Departmental coach is worthy of note, as are the yard lamps.

THE STEAM LOCOMOTIVE SHED

This picture could be called the 'twilight' of the steam shed, for there were only a few days left of BR steam when it was taken at Lostock Hall shed on the evening of 19 July 1968. Class 5MT 4-6-0 No 45110 is seen in the company of 8F 2-8-0s Nos 48294 and 48476 and also two unidentified 'Black Fives'. No 45110 worked the Liverpool-Manchester section of the BR '15 Guinea Special' on the following 11 August. Happily, it was subsequently preserved by the Stanier Black Five Locomotive Preservation Society at the Severn Valley Railway, Bridgnorth, and has seen much work on main-line charter trains.

OUTSIDE VIEW

Above On the evening of 12 September 1986, ex-LNWR Webb Class 2F 0-6-0 'Coal Tank' No 1054 is seen at the remains of the former GWR shed at Worcester (85A). By this time only one of the two large shed buildings remained and a few outbuildings where No 1054 was being serviced prior to leaving for Kidderminster and the SVR. That day it had travelled to Worcester from Chester via Shrewsbury and Hereford.

Above right Here is another pre-Grouping locomotive, this time ex-Caledonian Railway Class 2P 0-4-4 tank No 55216, in the tiny shed at Kyle of Lochalsh on 3 May 1957. Unlike the Webb 'Coal Tank', which was built around 1882, No 55216 was comparatively youthful, having been built at St Rollox Works in Glasgow in 1912. Note the shed's stone construction. *Hugh Ballantyne*

Right To complete this trio of veteran engines, we travel across the Irish Sea to the Isle of Man, where, on the afternoon of 29 August 1974, Beyer Peacock 2-4-0 tank No 10 *G. H. Wood* (in lined green livery) waits outside the tiny shed at Port Erin, prior to taking out the 1615 to Douglas. As with the Kyle picture, the stonework is worthy of note, as is the Manx name on the side of the shed. The lovely Beyer Peacock engines were introduced in the 1870s, and it's good to know that some of them are still running today.

THE STEAM LOCOMOTIVE SHED

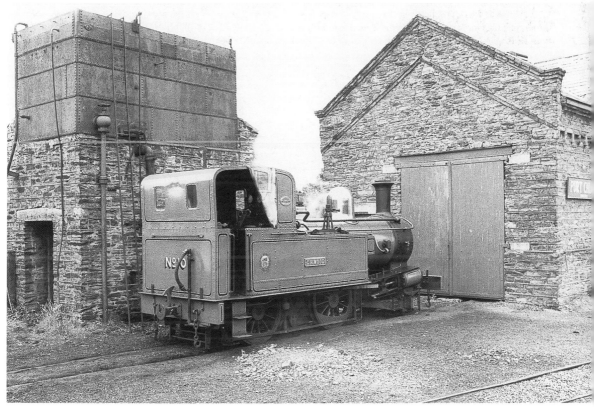

Above On the evening of 16 May 1957, ex-Midland Railway Class 3F 0-6-0 No 43645 basks in the sunshine outside the diminutive shed at Tewkesbury. At the time this locomotive was used mainly on the Ashchurch to Upton-on-Severn service, which was withdrawn in 1961. *Hugh Ballantyne*

Below In complete contrast, this is Heaton Mersey shed near Stockport on the evening of 24 April 1968, showing ex-LMS 8F 2-8-0s Nos 48170, 48171 and 48267, and 'Black Five' No 44868. The shed would be closed within a few weeks of this picture being taken.

THE STEAM LOCOMOTIVE SHED

Willesden shed (1A), some 5 miles from Euston, is the setting for our last picture in this section. Taken on 17 January 1965, it shows, from left to right, 8F 2-8-0s Nos 48624 (with earlier-type tender) and 48387, 'Black Fives' Nos 45001 and 44771, and 'Jinty' 0-6-0 tank No 47435, behind which is No 47432 of the same class, plus a packed yard of locomotives, mainly 8Fs and 5MTs, with some BR Standard designs. Willesden was mainly a freight depot with a few passenger locomotives allocated to it. It closed in September 1965 and after demolition became the site for a Freightliner terminal. *Hugh Ballantyne*

3.
SERVICING

Below The last Maunsell U Class 2-6-0 in service is seen over the ashpits by the coaling stage at Guildford on 8 June 1966. On the extreme right is the edge of the tender of the last N Class 'Mogul' in service, No 31408. I was lucky to obtain pictures of these engines as they had officially been taken out of service on 5 June, and were in fact withdrawn shortly after this picture was taken. I travelled to Guildford overnight after a 'gig' in Birmingham, and as my Mini was out of action I was fortunate to be able to use my father's Vauxhall Victor for the journey, with its column gear change and bench seats. I always thought the BR 'Lion and Wheel' emblem, seen here, was attractive. Note also the locomotive power classification on the cab side – '4P 3F'.

Bottom In 1919 the GWR purchased from the Government's Railway Operating Division several 2-8-0s locomotives. These powerful 'RODs', with their 32,200lb tractive effort, were ideal for heavy goods trains, and worked long into the 1950s. The design had originated with Robinson on the GCR in 1911, being used by the ROD during the First World War around 1917. On 19 August 1951 'ROD' No 3034 sits over the ashpits at St Philips Marsh shed, Bristol. *Hugh Ballantyne*

Class 5MT 4-6-0 No 45287 sits under the giant coaling stage at Rose Grove shed (10F) on 19 July 1968. This shed, to the west of Burnley on the Blackburn to Sowerby Bridge line, was one of the last to have an allocation of steam locomotives on BR.

SERVICING

Above Ex-GWR Class 5600 0-6-2 tank No 6697 stands over the ashpit at Croes Newydd shed on Saturday 7 May 1966. Seven examples of this tank engine, which was designed for service in the Welsh valleys, have been preserved, including No 6697 at the GW Society headquarters at Didcot.

Below At one time Banbury shed boasted ash-dropping shelters; however, when this picture was taken on 26 February 1966 very little of them seems to remain. Receiving attention at the ashpits are 'Black Five' 4-6-0 No 45331 and BR Standard Class 9F 2-10-0 No 92212. Banbury shed closed the following September.

THE STEAM LOCOMOTIVE SHED

A brace of 9F 2-10-0s, Nos 92101 and 92102, get ready to leave the coaling area at Stoke shed on the evening of Sunday 24 April 1966. Unlike the Banbury shed of old, the ashpits here seem to be completely open to the elements.

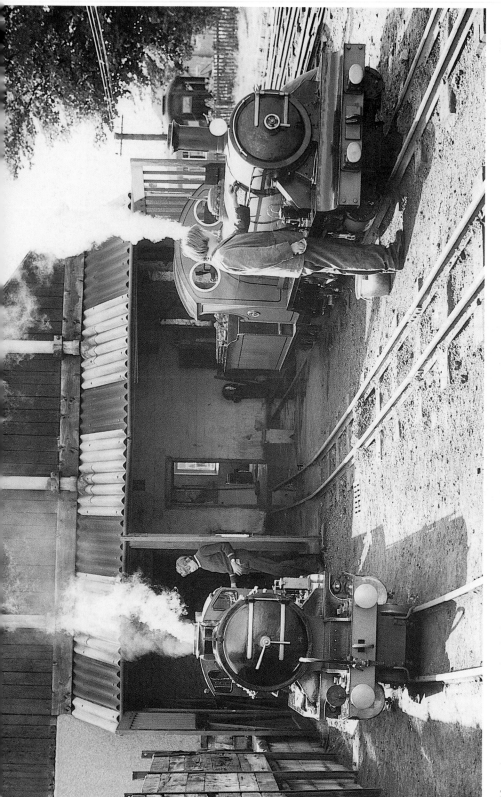

Above A sunny summer morning, 21 August 1975, at Ravenglass shed on the 15-inch-gauge Ravenglass & Eskdale Railway. *River Mite* (left) and *River Irt* are receiving a final check-up before the day's work, taking holidaymakers on the 7-mile journey to Dalegarth in the shadow of Eskdale Fell in the heart of the Lake District. The older of the two locomotives, *River Irt*, is a rebuild of *Muriel*, an 0-8-0 tank dating from 1894. The 0-8-2 entered service in 1928. *River Mite*, a 2-8-2, was built by H. Clarkson & Sons of York for the R&ER Preservation Society Ltd and entered service in May 1967.

Below Ex-North British Railway Class J37 0-6-0 No 64602 takes water at Dundee Tay Bridge shed on 22 June 1966 as ex-LMS Ivatt Class 2MT 2-6-0 No 46464 looks on. This 'Mogul' has been preserved and works on the Strathspey Railway at Aviemore, but sadly none of the J37s survived into preservation.

THE STEAM LOCOMOTIVE SHED

Above Tyseley shed (originally 84E in Western Region days, then 2A on transfer to the LMR) was opened in 1908, and when it closed to steam in November 1966 it was still home to the last three GWR pannier tank locomotives in service. It provided power for local suburban services as well as goods trains and shunting duties. The last GWR-type 'Castle' Class 4-6-0, No 7029 (formerly *Clun Castle*), is still on BR books as it receives attention at the shed on 15 May 1966 before working to Banbury on a parcels train. Like Tyseley, which is now a working museum, No 7029 was preserved (at that Birmingham shed) and has seen much work on the main line over the years. At the back of the locomotive can be seen part of the large shed, which housed two 65-foot turntables, each with 28 bays, plus a 12-road repair shop.

Below The driver of Class 5MT No 44938 oils round his machine prior to leaving Willesden shed yard on 10 June 1964. *Hugh Ballantyne*

One of the shed fitters works on the unusual Caprotti valve gear cylinders of BR Standard Class 5MT 4-6-0 No 73128 at Manchester Patricroft shed (9H) on the afternoon of Saturday 18 November 1967. This and Newton Heath (9D) were the last two sheds in the Manchester area to have a steam allocation, and both had closed by the end of June 1968.

SERVICING

THE STEAM LOCOMOTIVE SHED

Above left On 4 October 1966 ex-LMS 8F 2-8-0 No 48697 is seen near Croes Newydd shed with a load of coal for the GWR-type coaler, which can be seen on the right of the picture, and next to which are several stored engines including pannier tanks, a 'Black Five' and an 8F.

Left Conversation piece at Buxton shed (9L) on the afternoon of Friday 20 May 1966, as Ivatt Class 2MT 2-6-0 No 46465 prepares to leave the shed after being coaled and watered. The edge of the shed building can just be seen to the left of the locomotive. This former LNWR shed opened in 1892, and in the mid-1950s had an allocation of around 50 locomotives. It closed in March 1968.

Above For many years the 'shed goat' at Guildford was ex-USA 0-6-0 tank locomotive No 30072 (see also page 37). On 8 June 1966 No 30072 and diesel shunter No D2288 head out of the shed area. No 30072 is now preserved on the Keighley & Worth Valley Railway at Haworth.

SERVICING

These two pictures show a complete contrast in coaling methods. The first, taken at Aberdeen's Ferryhill shed (61B) on Tuesday 14 June 1966, shows one of Sir Nigel Gresley's legendary A4 Class 'Pacific' locomotives, No 60034 *Lord Faringdon*, being coaled in readiness to take out the 1.30pm Aberdeen-Glasgow train, the 'Grampian'. That year was to be the 'Indian summer' of this famous class; they were withdrawn from service by September of that year. Six members of the class were preserved, but alas not No 60034.

From one of Gresley's finest to the vintage Beyer Peacock locomotives that run on the 3-foot-gauge Isle of Man Railway. No 13 *Kissack* is seen being coaled by hand at Douglas on 30 August 1974. In the background can be seen the shed building.

THE STEAM LOCOMOTIVE SHED

Below On 22 July 1975 veteran LNWR 2-4-0 No 790 *Hardwicke*, built in 1892, is seen coaling in Carnforth shed yard prior to making a trial run over the Furness line to Sellafield and return in readiness for its appearance at the Rail 150 celebrations at Shildon at the end of August 1975. No 790 was active again in the summer of the following year with a series of shuttle trips between Carnforth and Grange-over-Sands.

Right Unrebuilt SR 'West Country' Class 4-6-2 No 34092 *City of Wells* is a long way from home as it receives attention at Carlisle Upperby shed on 30 April 1983. It had just worked into Carlisle over the Settle & Carlisle route with a special charter train, the 'Cumbrian Mountain Express'. Although now a diesel depot, Upperby is regularly used for servicing the many preserved steam locomotives that work to Carlisle on special trains.

Below BR Standard Class 4MT 2-6-0 No 76095 stands in the coaling bay at Chester shed (6A) on the afternoon of 24 April 1966. The locomotive was built at Harwich Works in 1957 and withdrawn from service in March 1967.

THE STEAM LOCOMOTIVE SHED

4.
THE SHED YARD

Above left and above It was always a joy to walk round a shed yard – you never knew what you were going to see. While on a trip to York on 1 May 1966 to see *Flying Scotsman* pay a visit to that Roman city, I visited not only the shed but also had a look round the shed yard, and on that sunny Sunday was rewarded with (*left*) the sight of one of Gresley's handsome V2 Class 2-6-2s, No 60886. These were introduced by the LNER in 1936 for use on express passenger trains and fast goods services such as the pre-war 'Scotch Goods', the 3.40pm ex-Kings Cross Goods Depot. Their classification was 7P6F. Happily No 60800 *Green Arrow* (originally No 4771) is preserved and sees work on the main line. As if in contrast to the sleek lines of No 60886, behind it is one of the ex-LMS Ivatt-designed Class 4MT 2-6-0s. In front of the V2 is the tender of Class J27 0-6-0 No 65894.

Also in the yard that day (*above*) was the last ex-LNER Class A1 'Pacific' in service, No 60145, which was withdrawn shortly after this date. None of this class remain in preservation; however, one is being built, thanks to the efforts of the North Eastern Locomotive Preservation Group (NELPG).

Below left Another find was on a snowy 2 April 1966 at Wakefield shed (56A) yard, this time ex-LMS 'Jubilee' Class 4-6-0 No 45739 *Ulster*. These popular 4-6-0s were designed by Sir William Stanier and introduced in 1934. Four examples are preserved, Nos 45593, 45596, 45690 and 45699.

THE SHED YARD

To quote the photographer, it was a 'delightful surprise' to find this ex-Midland Railway 0-4-0 tank in the shed yard at Swansea East Dock (87D) on 19 May 1964; note the bell by the cab window. This class was introduced in 1907 and designed by Deeley. Behind the locomotive is an ex-GWR Class 5600 0-6-2 tank, flanked by a pair of 0-6-0 pannier tanks. *Hugh Ballantyne*

THE STEAM LOCOMOTIVE SHED

On 17 May 1966 ex-LMS 0-4-0 saddle tank No 47000 rests near Sheep Pasture shed on the Cromford & High Peak line. These chunky-looking 0-4-0STs were introduced in 1932 to a Kitson design prepared to Stanier's requirements. In the background is the winding house at the top of the Sheep Pasture incline.

Above The low winter sun highlights the sleek lines and Walschaerts valve gear of BR Standard Class 4MT 4-6-0 No 75033 as it stands in the shed yard at Croes Newydd on 13 March 1967.

Below Not quite Saltley shed yard (21A then 2E), but near enough to use as an excuse to show 'Coronation' Class 'Pacific' No 46235 *City of Birmingham* as it waits to enter the shed area on 19 May 1966, prior to being put on display at the Birmingham Science Museum the following Sunday (22 May).

Right It is the early evening of Sunday 11 August 1968 and I was looking round Carnforth shed yard after photographing the very last BR steam train, the '15 Guinea Special' return working from Carlisle via the Settle & Carlisle to Liverpool Lime Street. There were many locomotives in the yard, mostly awaiting scrapping (see page 127), but there were several exceptions, including BR Standard Class 4MT 4-6-0 No 75027, seen here. The 4-6-0, which was destined for preservation on the Bluebell Railway in Sussex, found regular work right until the end of steam, mainly on the Grassington branch, along with sister engine No 75019, which, unlike No 75027, was scrapped. Also visible in the picture is the front end of ex-LMS Fairburn Class 4MT 2-6-4 tank No 42085, destined for preservation on the Lakeside Railway at Haverthwaite.

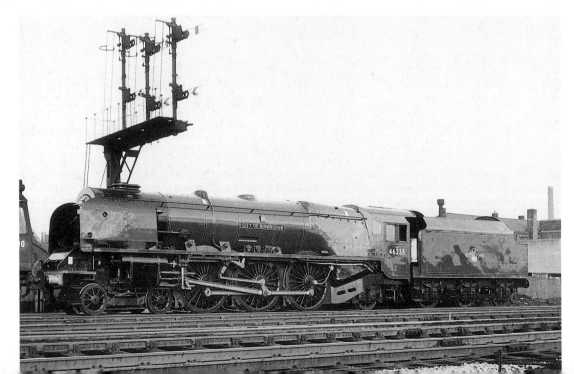

THE SHED YARD

Above Class 5 4-6-0s Nos 45095 and 45394 prepare to leave Carnforth shed on 16 April 1968 for shunting duties in the nearby goods yard, situated by the Furness line to Grange and Barrow. They would also probably make trip workings along the coast route, which saw steam workings right until the end of BR steam.

Left The external condition of Class 5MT No 44703 makes a striking contrast with the locomotives in the previous picture. The smart-looking 4-6-0 is standing in the yard at its home shed, Ferryhill (61B), at Aberdeen on 14 June 1966 next to the shed breakdown set.

Right Another 'Black Five' 4-6-0, this time No 45073, is seen in the yard at its home shed, Lostock Hall (10D), on the evening of 19 July 1968. Facing it is 4-6-0 No 44888. In the last weeks of BR steam these 4-6-0s, together with 8F 2-8-0s, could be found at work with coal traffic on the Preston-Blackburn-Burnley route.

THE STEAM LOCOMOTIVE SHED

This next photograph provides a fine view of Carlisle Upperby (12B) shed yard on 30 August 1964. On display are ex-LMS 'Princess Royal' 'Pacific' No 46200 *The Princess Royal* (stored), 9F 2-10-0 No 92006, 'Jinty' 0-6-0 tank No 47295, and Ivatt Class 2MT 2-6-0 No 46426. In the background are 'Royal Scot' 4-6-0 No 46110

Grenadier Guardsman and ex-LMS 'Patriot' Class 4-6-0 No 45545 *Planet*, to the right of which is an Ivatt Class 4MT 2-6-0. Approaching this splendid collection is another unidentified 'Royal Scot' 4-6-0. *Hugh Ballantyne*

THE STEAM LOCOMOTIVE SHED

Above A trio of ex-LMS Fairburn Class 4MT 2-6-4 tanks are on display in the yard at Neasden (Great Central) locomotive shed on 9 September 1961. As well as Nos 42080, 42070 and 42291 there is ex-LMS Fowler 2-6-0 ('Crab') No 42747 and a breakdown crane. With its close proximity to Wembley, on Cup Final days and other sporting occasions Neasden shed would see a lot of activity with locomotive types from many Regions turning up at the shed for servicing. *Hugh Ballantyne*

Below To follow that trio of Fairburn tanks, here are three ex-LMS 8F 2-8-0s on display in the yard at Stourton shed on a wintry 2 April 1966. No 48093 heads the parade with Nos 48311 and 48126 completing the scene. Some of the many chimneys of the shed building can be seen on the left. The 8Fs were also known among spotters as 'Consols', which was short for 'Consolidation', the name applied to locos with a 2-8-0 wheel arrangement. They were designed by Stanier and introduced in 1935, and lasted until the very end of steam.

THE STEAM LOCOMOTIVE SHED

Left On 19 July 1968 8F 2-8-0 No 48400 is seen in Rose Grove shed yard in the company of two Type 2 Bo-Bo diesels (later Class 25), which would of course in a few days' time help to oust steam traction from BR.

Above Wigan Springs Branch shed (8F) had closed to steam on 4 December 1967, but while on a visit to the North West from 25 to 27 February 1968 in search of steam, I learned from a chat on the lineside that there was still a quantity of locomotives in the yard awaiting disposal. So before returning to Birmingham on the late afternoon of 27 February, I visited the yard, and as you can see I was not disappointed. Several dozen locomotives were

on display, including 'Black Fives', 8Fs, BR 'Britannias' and BR 4-6-0s and 2-6-0s. Also of interest are the parked A35 Austin van and Ford Anglia.

Below In March 1966 'Britannia' 'Pacific' No 70016 (formerly *Ariel*) runs through Carlisle Kingmoor shed yard and is about to pass ex-Midland Railway Class 3F 'Jinty' 0-6-0 tank No 47531 and ex-LMS 'Royal Scot' Class 4-6-0 No 46115 *Scots Guardsman*, the last of the class in service, and now preserved alongside with No 46100 *Royal Scot*. Note the stripe on the cab of No 46115 to denote that this locomotive is barred from working south of Crewe, due to limited clearance beneath the new overhead electric wires.

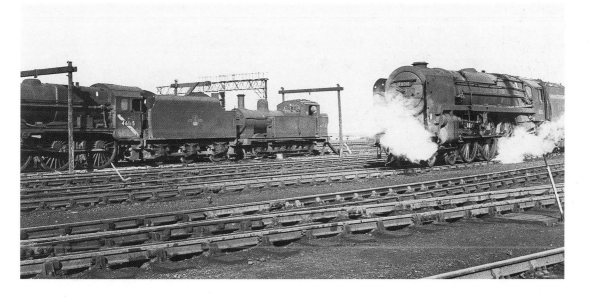

THE SHED YARD

Above When I visited the east of Scotland in June 1966, there were still a number of Gresley Class J38 0-6-0s at work around Thornton in the Kingdom of Fife. Thornton shed (62A) was probably the final home for these sturdy looking goods locomotives, and a visit to the shed yard on the morning of Thursday 16 June produced this picture of No 65921. Alas, none of the class survived into preservation.

Below An engine that did survive into preservation was former NER Class J27 0-6-0 No 65894, seen here at York shed on 1 May 1966. Today this locomotive can be seen at work on the North Yorkshire Moors Railway, numbered 2392. It is also a star of TV, being featured in the titles of the popular drama series *Heartbeat*, which is set in the glorious North Yorkshire Moors National Park area. Note the snow plough attached to the front of the loco.

THE STEAM LOCOMOTIVE SHED

Another veteran locomotive is former NBR Class J36 0-6-0 No 65345, seen here being used as a stationary boiler at Thornton shed, also on 16 June 1966. One member of these handsome engines survives today, No 673 (65243) *Maude*. They were first introduced in 1888 and designed by Holmes.

THE STEAM LOCOMOTIVE SHED

Opposite page The yard at Crewe South shed on the early evening of 24 April 1966 is the setting as one of the powerful BR Standard 9F 2-10-0s, No 92002, heads a line of locomotives including an Ivatt Class 2MT 2-6-0 and another 9F. No 92002 was among the first 9Fs built, entering service in January 1954. It was withdrawn in November 1967, having had one of the longest lives of this generally short-lived yet illustrious class. Note the shed code, 2A, which at the time denoted Tyseley.

Also at Crewe South on the same evening was Standard Class 2 2-6-0 No 78019, which today is preserved at the Severn Valley Railway at Bridgnorth.

Above Looking very woebegone without its coupling rods and valve gear, and bereft of its nameplate, is unrebuilt 'Battle of Britain' 'Pacific' No 34076, formerly *41 Squadron*. The location is Salisbury shed yard on the morning of Thursday 7 April 1966.

Below A line-up of Wainwright-design ex-SECR Class R1 0-6-0 tanks at Folkestone shed (74C) on 15 March 1959. Their numbers are 31107, 31010, 31047 and 31128. These locomotives were used for work on the heavy boat trains up the Folkestone Harbour branch to Folkestone Junction. Note the cut-down cab on No 31010; this locomotive had originally been used on the Canterbury to Whitstable goods-only branch line, which had a restricted loading gauge and had closed in 1953. *Hugh Ballantyne*

5.
COALING PLANTS

Above and above right At one time, with the number of locomotive sheds in the UK, some of the coaling plants (or stages) must have stood out in the surrounding areas like church towers. This seemed to be especially so in northern England. However, in the south and west of the country, dominated by the old Southern Railway and the GWR, the coaling stage seemed to be much more compact and, particularly with the Great Western, of a more uniform design. This is certainly illustrated in these two pictures, the first at Banbury shed on 13 August 1966, with Class 5 4-6-0 No 45051 by the coaling stage, a typical GWR structure supporting a large water tank. Examples of this type could be found all over the system, including the next picture, taken at what is thought to be Tyseley shed in the mid-1950s, showing one of the handsome-looking GWR 'Castle' Class 4-6-0s, No 5071 *Spitfire*, waiting its turn for replenishment. *RS/RS collection*

THE STEAM LOCOMOTIVE SHED

In complete contrast to the previous pictures is this scene on the North Eastern Region at Royston shed (55D) on 3 April 1966, with No 45207 standing in the shed yard near the coaler.

I mentioned that some coaling stages must have stood out like church spires or towers, and this was probably the case at Carnforth. The first picture was taken there on the evening of 10 April 1982, and shows beautifully preserved ex-LMS 'Coronation Pacific' No 46229 *Duchess of Hamilton* by one of the two massive coaling plants, still there today. Behind the 4-6-2 is ex-Lancashire & Yorkshire Railway 0-6-0 No 1300 (BR No 52322). That day No 44229 had worked into Carnforth with a special charter from Leeds.

In the second picture ex-Somerset & Dorset Railway Class 7F 2-8-0 No 13809 (BR No 53809) makes a fine sight on the morning of 30 April 1983. Both Carnforth's impressive-looking coaling towers can be seen; note also the huge water tower. No 13809 was being serviced prior to taking out the first leg of the 'Cumbrian Mountain Pullman' train between Carnforth and Hellifield, from where 'West Country' 'Pacific' *City of Wells* would take the train forward over the S&C to Carlisle (see page 63).

THE STEAM LOCOMOTIVE SHED

A busy scene at Grantham shed (34F) on 3 August 1963 with, from left to right, Class B1 4-6-0 No 61392, Class A3 'Pacific' No 60048 *Doncaster* (complete with smoke deflectors), two WD Class 2-8-0s and WD Class 2-8-0 No 90032 on the coal stage road, all overlooked by the very high coaling plant. *Hugh Ballantyne*

THE STEAM LOCOMOTIVE SHED

A similar coaling stage to that at Grantham was to be found at Dundee Tay Bridge shed. After filling its eight-wheeled tender with coal, A2 'Pacific' No 60530 *Sayajirao* moves back on to the shed to carry on its duties as standby locomotive on 17 June 1966. Note the inspection pit in the foreground.

THE STEAM LOCOMOTIVE SHED

The coaling tower at Rose Grove shed was impressive, and could certainly be seen in the surrounding countryside. These two views were taken at almost the end of its active life, on 19 July 1968, with ex-LMS Stanier Class 8F 2-8-0s Nos 48167 and 48728 waiting by the side of the coaler. Note the ladders required to gain access to the top; you would need to be fit to negotiate them! Also note the somewhat intricate lighting system.

COALING PLANTS

Compared with those of other members of the 'Big Four', some of the Southern Railway's coaling plants appeared to be rather ramshackle affairs. Witness this coaler at Guildford, which was set away from the shed area and, as can be seen, next to Guildford station. On 8 June 1966 ex-SR N Class 2-6-0 No 31408 moves away from the coaling plant area in the direction of the shed, leaving U Class 'Mogul' No 31639 on the coal road, and another unidentified locomotive just behind. Note also the very long covered footbridge at the rear of the picture, which runs from the station and passes over the goods yard, etc, before exiting into a nearby road. These long covered footbridges, which were a feature of the Southern Railway, could be found at other large stations, including Exeter Central.

THE STEAM LOCOMOTIVE SHED

Normanton shed (55E) near Wakefield in the West Riding of Yorkshire is the location as Ivatt Class 4MT 2-6-0 No 43129 pauses in its shunting duties beneath one of the shed's two coaling stages on the morning of Sunday 3 April 1966. Normanton's coaler makes an interesting comparison with that at Guildford.

THE STEAM LOCOMOTIVE SHED

Above left A bleak scene at Farnley Junction shed near Leeds on Saturday 2 April 1966. Ex-LMS Stanier 'Jubilee' Class 4-6-0 No 45581 *Bihar and Orissa* is being coaled during an unseasonable snowstorm, after which it returned to the comparative comfort of the loco shed (see page 13).

Left Ex-GCR Robinson Class O4 2-8-0 No 63644 and ex-LNER Class B1 4-6-0 No 61145 pose for the camera in Colwick shed yard on Sunday 20 March 1966.

Overshadowing them is the high coaling tower. Next to the O4 is the front end of another O4, No 63675, and behind the row of ex-LNER locomotives are 8F and 'Black Five' intruders.

Above For a few seconds on a misty Manchester November day in 1967 (the 18th) the sun came out and highlighted Patricroft shed as 8F 2-8-0 No 48617 ran off the shed and passed the neat-looking coaling tower.

COALING PLANTS

THE STEAM LOCOMOTIVE SHED

Left On 11 August 1968, ex-LMS Class 5 4-6-0 No 45390 rests in the yard in Carnforth next to one of the giant coaling towers, which at first glance looks like the bridge of a ship. Several 'Black Fives' have been preserved, but No 45390 was not one of the lucky ones.

Above Another engine that was not spared the breaker's torch was 8F 2-8-0 No 48400, seen here on the afternoon of Sunday 25 February 1968 near the coaling plant at Lostock Hall.

COALING PLANTS

6.
PASSING BY

Above This is Pembroke Dock shed, as seen from the 3.50pm to Whitland, hauled by ex-GWR Class 4500 2-6-2 tank No 5520 on 8 June 1960. Outside this small sub-shed of Neyland (87H) is one of numerous ex-GWR Class 51XX 4MT 2-6-2 tanks, No 4107. At one time these larger Prairie tank engines could be found almost anywhere on the GWR system. Fortunately, several members of the class have been preserved, as have examples of the lighter 4500 Class. *Hugh Ballantyne*

Above right On 18 November 1967 8F 2-8-0 heads past Newton Heath shed in the suburbs of Manchester with a southbound mixed goods.

Right From the footbridge that led to Wakefield shed, a good view was obtained not only of the shed area but also of the line from Pontefract, which in 1966 still generated a fair amount of steam-hauled freight traffic. On the evening of Thursday 26 May of that year, ex-WD 8F 2-8-0 No 90210 heads for Wakefield with a heavy-looking coal train. Note the abundance of semaphore signals still in use in the area.

THE STEAM LOCOMOTIVE SHED

On the evening of Saturday 7 May 1983 'Peak' Class Type 4 diesel-electric No 45150 heads north out of Wellingborough with the 1650 from St Pancras to Sheffield. Behind the train is the diesel depot, built near the steam shed (15A), which can be seen in the right background; note also the water tank, surviving from steam days. On the depot are a pair of Class 47s and a Class 31. With the end of the winter timetable in 1983, the popular 'Peaks' gave way to HSTs on this route, and many of them were transferred to the North Wales coast route for service between Manchester and Bangor/Holyhead. By the late 1980s they had been withdrawn from service.

THE STEAM LOCOMOTIVE SHED

The diesel depot at Leicester is on the site of the old Leicester Midland steam shed (15C). On 3 June 1987 *Flying Scotsman* passes the depot and heads for Leicester London Road station with the empty stock of a special charter train returning from Leicester to Dorridge. This special train was one of a series running that week between Dorridge and Leicester, organised by Cromwell Engineering, hence the 'Cromwell Pullman' nameboard. There is plenty to interest the traction enthusiast with a variety of diesel locos on shed, including Classes 20, 40, 45 and the ubiquitous Class 47. Also poking its nose out of the repair shop is a Class 31.

THE STEAM LOCOMOTIVE SHED

Above left English Electric Class 37 No 37407 heads out of Holyhead on the afternoon of 31 August 1995 with the 1553 service to Crewe. In the background is the site of the former shed (6J), which as can be seen was by then a diesel servicing depot. Note also the mixture of semaphore and colour light signalling, and also the signal box. As with the earlier scene at Wellingborough, the Class 37s have now been superseded on this route by new types of diesel units, thus eliminating another set of loco-hauled trains.

Left The former LB&SCR station at Tunbridge Wells West is the setting as Class 207 East Sussex three-car unit No 1317 pulls out with the 1012 to Eridge. This view clearly shows the former shed building (75F), albeit bereft of trackwork. The building was demolished some years ago, but the station and line, which were closed, have now been preserved. This picture was taken from the signal box on 31 August 1983 by kind permission of the signalman.

Above Another steam shed that has been turned into a diesel servicing area is at Worcester. On 17 June 1983 a pair of Class 20s, Nos 20147 and 20169, run past the remains of the old shed buildings with the 1245 Bescot-Gloucester goods. Today nothing remains of the shed buildings, but the servicing area is still there, used mainly by the many DMUs that abound in the area. Also still there are the fine-looking GWR-type semaphore signals.

THE STEAM LOCOMOTIVE SHED

The next two scenes will evoke memories of the much-loved Somerset & Dorset Joint Railway, which ran between Bath and Bournemouth. The line was closed on 7 March 1966, but, I am sure, will never be forgotten. Radstock, some 10 miles south of Bath, is our first location, where we see Standard 4MT 2-6-0 No 76027 leaving for Bath with the 12.05pm from Templecombe. On the left is the neat-looking locomotive shed, which housed small tank engines for shunting at the local collieries and also for banking goods trains up the 7½ miles to Masbury summit, south of Radstock. This picture was taken from the then recently closed Radstock A signal box on 3 April 1965.

The second picture shows Standard Class 5MT No 73054, having reversed out of Templecombe, heading south at Templecombe Lower with the 9.03am Bristol to Bournemouth West train on 27 July 1963. Stored on the right is ex-GWR Collett Class 3MT 0-6-0 No 3215. In the middle distance can be seen the back of Templecombe shed, to the right of which is the turntable and shed yard. Note also in the top left-hand corner the line leading to Templecombe Upper.
Both Hugh Ballantyne

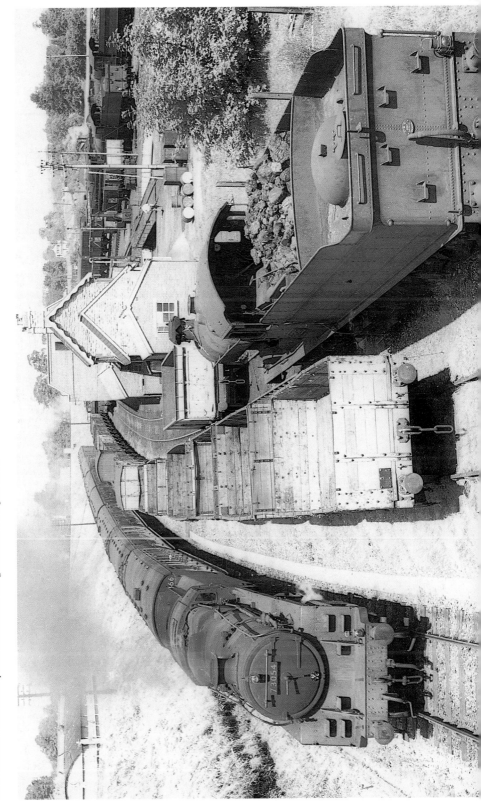

Above On Thursday 21 July 1966 I had spent a very enjoyable day on the Isle of Wight's railways, having travelled to the island by ferry from Lymington Dock. Returning to Lymington Dock that evening, I caught the 7.15pm to Brockenhurst, alighting at Lymington Town station, where I took this picture of the train engine, Ivatt Class 2MT 2-6-2 tank No 41316 as it waited to pull out for Brockenhurst. Prominent in the background is the small loco shed, a sub-shed of Eastleigh (71A), which housed the branch locomotives. Note also the typical rail-built SR semaphore signal.

Below A busy scene at Newton Abbot on the early evening of Sunday 7 July 1985, as English Electric Class 50 No 50030 *Repulse* approaches platform No 3 with the 1727 Paignton to Birmingham New Street train. In platform No 2, being watched by a large crowd, are 'Castle' Class 4-6-0 No 5051 *Drysllwyn Castle* and 'Hall' Class 4-6-0 No 4930 *Hagley Hall*, with a Taunton-Plymouth special train in connection with the GWR 150 celebrations of that year. In the upper right of the picture can be seen the diesel MPD, built on the site of the old steam shed (see page 43). The GWR signal box, signal gantry and mass of trackwork complete this sunny railway scene. Alas, by 1987 the box, gantry and some of the trackwork had disappeared.

THE STEAM LOCOMOTIVE SHED

7.
TURNTABLES

Left Surrounded by 'Black Five' 4-6-0s and 8F 2-8-0s, including No 44690, Stanier 2-8-0 No 48723 is turned on the vacuum-powered turntable at Rose Grove shed on 19 July 1968; note the pipe connecting the loco and turntable.

Above right A smoky scene at Melton Constable (32G) on 29 August 1958, as Class J17 0-6-0 No 65567 is turned on the Ransomes & Rapier turntable, with Ivatt 2-6-0 No 43156 looking on. In the background are the shed buildings. The J17s were first introduced at the beginning of the 1900s, and were designed by Holden for the Great Eastern Railway. Much has been written about Melton Constable over the years, but suffice to say that it was a very important cross-country junction, set in rural northern Norfolk. It was also the site of the Midland & Great Northern Joint Railway works. Some of its busiest times were on summer Saturdays, with many trains from the Midlands and northern England to the popular resorts of Cromer and Yarmouth. Melton Constable was a victim of the many closures in Norfolk in the early 1960s. *Hugh Ballantyne*

Right No 34006 *Bude*, one of Bulleid's unrebuilt 'West Country' 'Pacific' locomotives, is seen on the turntable at Salisbury shed on 7 April 1966.

THE STEAM LOCOMOTIVE SHED

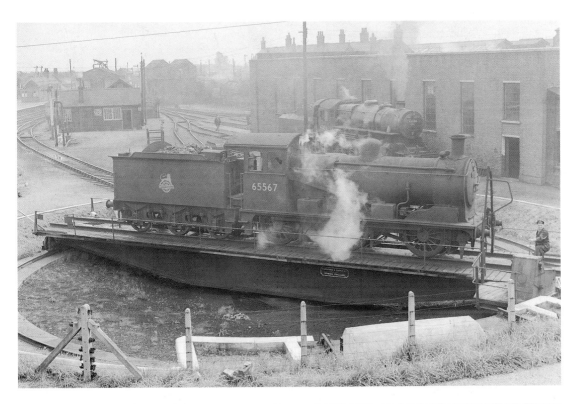

THE STEAM LOCOMOTIVE SHED

Above Some locomotive sheds were roundhouses complete with their own turntables. This was certainly the case at many GWR depots, large and small, from the massive Old Oak Common shed with its four roundhouses to sheds like Croes Newydd, near Wrexham, with just one. Former GWR 0-6-2 tank No 6697 is seen on the turntable at Croes Newydd on the afternoon of Saturday 7 May 1966. Behind is 0-6-0 pannier tank No 1628.

Below Dundee Tay Bridge was another shed with a vacuum-powered turntable, and ex-LNER Gresley Class V2 2-6-2 No 60919 was photographed being turned on it on Friday 17 June 1966. Not all turntables were vacuum-powered, however; many locomotives had to be turned manually, although for some lucky crews there were electrically controlled examples.

Above Today there are very few turntables left on BR. One is at Perth goods yard, north of the station, and after working to Perth from Edinburgh on a Forth Bridge centenary special train on 4 March 1990, A4 'Pacific' No 60009 is turned by hand, which as you can see required the efforts of several men.

Below One hand seems to be all that is required to turn RHDR 4-6-2 No 8 *Hurricane*, seen here on the turntable at New Romney on 16 August 1969.

THE STEAM LOCOMOTIVE SHED

Another location that still boasts a turntable is at 'Steamtown' Carnforth shed. On 1 May 1976 LNWR 2-4-0 No 790 *Hardwicke* is being turned while No 4472, after being turned, is waiting to couple up to No 790 so that they can work a special charter train to Hellifield in connection with the Settle & Carlisle centenary. At that time, the S&C was not approved for steam running, which did not come about until 1978.

Another picture at Carnforth, this time on 7 November 1981, as LNER Class K1 2-6-0 No 2005 is photographed on the yard turntable prior to working out with a southbound charter train, the 'Trans Pennine Pullman'. This special was hauled from Carnforth to Leeds by No 2005, then from Leeds to Northwich via Stalybridge by SR 'Lord Nelson' Class 4-6-0 No 850 *Lord Nelson*.

THE STEAM LOCOMOTIVE SHED

Yeovil Junction on the former SR's Waterloo to Exeter route still has a turntable, which, together with a maintenance building, is now part of the Yeovil Railway Centre. On Sunday 21 June 1992, SR Class N15 'King Arthur' 4-6-0 No 777 *Sir Lamiel* is turned at Yeovil Junction prior to running light to Exeter to return with an Exeter-Salisbury charter train, the outward working having been in the hands of 'West Country' 'Pacific' No 34027 *Taw Valley*. In the background of the Junction station is Class 47 diesel No 47526 on the 0755 Basingstoke-Exeter service.

The second scene shows the mighty looking GWR 'King' Class 4-6-0 No 6024 *King Edward I* about to be turned at Yeovil on 5 September 1998. It had earlier worked into Yeovil Pen Mill station (on the Weymouth line) with a special from Didcot. The special had been worked to Weymouth from Pen Mill by Class 47 diesel No 47721. Later that day, the 'King' would work the return special from Weymouth to Didcot. This modern-looking turntable has a continental look about it, reminding me of examples I have seen in West Germany.

8.
INDUSTRIAL SHEDS

Left Industrial locomotive sheds were rarely if ever on the same scale as BR, but nevertheless they were interesting places to visit, with very much the same servicing activities taking place as with their bigger brothers. On 2 April 1970 No 48, a Hunslet 0-6-0 saddle tank built in 1948, Works No 3685, takes water near Manvers Main colliery locomotive shed at Wath-on-Dearne, South Yorkshire.

Above On the same day, another Hunslet locomotive, this time 0-6-0 saddle tank No 49, built in 1950, Works No 3701, basks in the afternoon sunshine outside the modern-looking shed building.

Below In July 1972 I made two visits to the Birchenwood Gas & Coke Co Ltd near Kidsgrove in Staffordshire. On the second visit, on the 26 July, I was fortunate enough to photograph two locomotives outside the rather run-down-looking shed building. On the left is No 4, an outside-cylinder 0-6-0 saddle tank built by Bagnall in 1944 (Works No 2680). The second locomotive, another 0-6-0 saddle tank, No 5, although looking older than the Bagnall, was built in 1954 by Peckett (Works No 2153). The water tank is also worthy of note.

In the latter years of industrial steam, Mountain Ash colliery in South Wales was regarded as one of the 'Meccas' of industrial steam working, with an allocation of six locomotives, and usually two or three of them in steam on any working day. It also had a fair-sized locomotive shed, as this first scene, taken on 25 October 1972, shows. From left to right are Peckett 0-6-0 saddle tank *The Earl*, built in 1910 (Works No 1203), No 8, a Robert Stephenson & Hawthorns 0-6-0 saddle tank, built in 1944 (Works No 3880), and finally – pride of the shed – *Sir John*, an 0-6-0 saddle tank built by Avonside Engine Co in 1914 (Works No 1680) and rebuilt by them in 1929.

The second photograph, taken on 18 December 1972, shows *Sir John* outside the shed together with Llantanum Abbey, a Bagnall outside-cylinder 0-6-0 saddle tank built in 1939 (Works No 2074).

Finally, on 25 October 1972 No 8 receives attention outside Mountain Ash shed before setting off for another bout of shunting duties and a possible trip working to the phurnacite plant at Aberaman.

THE STEAM LOCOMOTIVE SHED

INDUSTRIAL SHEDS

The small railway complex at Stourport power station, in the heart of rural Worcestershire, was set on a high embankment with a connection to the nearby BR Severn Valley line just south of Stourport station, on the section to Hartlebury Junction. There were three locomotives 'on its books', with normally one or even two in steam daily, with one spare or under repair. On the late afternoon of 26 November 1972, the low sunlight highlights *WA No 2*, a Peckett 0-4-0 saddle tank of 1936 vintage (works No 1893) as it rests outside the neat-looking loco shed. The main duties for these locomotives were bringing coal trains up from the BR interchange sidings. The coal traffic had ceased by 1979, and by the early 1980s the power station had been demolished to make way for a housing estate.

THE STEAM LOCOMOTIVE SHED

On 20 November 1972 *Empress*, a Bagnall 0-6-0 saddle tank built in 1944, is seen inside the loco shed at Cadley Hill colliery near Burton-on-Trent. Behind *Empress* is another 0-6-0 saddle tank, *Progress*, which was built in 1946 by Robert Stephenson & Hawthorns (Works No 7298). The shed at Cadley Hill was a modern building, doubling, as was the case with many colliery sheds, as a workshop. As can be seen, it had two tracks with room for four locomotives. Cadley Hill also had a reputation for the cleanliness of its locomotives, which this picture well illustrates.

Above Outside Talywain locomotive shed on the morning of 18 December 1972 is *Islwyn*, an 0-6-0 saddle tank built in 1952 by Bagnalls of Stafford, Works No 2332. This large shed also served the nearby Blaenserchan Colliery.

Below A contrast to the previous picture, certainly in size, is this smart-looking engine shed at Maltby Main colliery in South Yorkshire. Outside the shed on 25 August 1967, being prepared for the day's work, is *Rothervale No 1*, an 0-6-0 saddle tank built in 1929 by the Yorkshire Engine Co (Works No 2240).

THE STEAM LOCOMOTIVE SHED

We conclude this section with a truly vintage locomotive, *Holwell No 3*, an 0-4-0 saddle tank built by Black Hawthorn in 1873 (Works No 266), sitting by the shed at Wirksworth Quarry (Bown & Shaw Ltd) on 23 February 1971, after completing its morning's work. Behind the veteran locomotive, which at the time was the oldest working steam loco in the country, is a comparative youngster of 1912 vintage,

Uppingham, an 0-4-0 saddle tank built by Peckett & Sons Ltd, Works No 1257. Note the shed building, obviously built of local stone.

These last three pictures demonstrate the wide variety of styles to be seen in industrial locomotive shed designs.

INDUSTRIAL SHEDS

9.
THE NEW AGE

This page We finish this book with a look at the 'new age' or modern diesel depots that have been built on the sites of, or close to, old steam sheds. The first two scenes were taken at Plymouth Laira depot on 3 April 1985, by kind permission of BR.

The first picture shows Class 50 No 50006 *Neptune*, a Class 47, another Class 50 and an 08 diesel shunter outside the distinctive-looking shed building.

In the second photograph Class 50 No 50041 *Bulwark* awaits its next turn of duty, surrounded by a variety of wheels. Laira, which also has a busy maintenance workshop as well as the general shed area, was opened in 1962 near the site of the steam shed (83D), which closed in 1964. The latter was then demolished, and is now the site of the staff car park, and also storage sidings.

Right Another famous locomotive shed, this time in the North of England, which is now a diesel and electric depot, is Carlisle Kingmoor (formerly 12A). On 30 April 1983 English Electric Class 40 No 40052 comes face-to-face with a Class 47 as it peers out of the depot.

THE STEAM LOCOMOTIVE SHED

This was the scene at Severn Tunnel Junction diesel depot on the evening of 25 September 1985. On shed are English Electric Class 37s, from front to back, Nos 37902, 37197, 37099 and 37285, together with several Class 08 shunters and two further unidentified Class 37s. Approaching from the left on an eastbound train of wagons is No 37426. The old steam shed (see page 40) was to the east of this location near the junction of the Gloucester and Swindon lines.

THE STEAM LOCOMOTIVE SHED

Leicester MPD is on the site of the former Leicester (Midland) loco shed (15A). This picture, taken with a telephoto lens on 2 July 1983, shows a wide variety of diesel locomotives on the depot with, from left to right, a row of Class 20s headed by No 20153, a pair of 08 shunters, Class 40 No 40095 together with two Class 25s, Class 46 No 46028, Class 31 No 31204 with a Class 47 behind, and No 47525, behind which is a Class 31 and Class 45 'Peak' diesel. At that time the Class 20s were regularly used in pairs on the Leicester-Skegness trains. Note also on the left-hand side the semaphore signals that were still in use in the Leicester area.

The old steam shed at Machynlleth (89C) in mid-Wales was still in use on 24 May 1987 as a DMU depot, albeit without its roof. When the second picture was taken on 18 April 1998, the main shed building had finally been demolished and the remaining area had been refurbished.

THE STEAM LOCOMOTIVE SHED

Right This scene, taken on 26 April 1984, shows Class 33 No 33038 departing from platform No 6 at Exeter St Davids with the 1425 to Paignton. On the left can be seen the remains of the steam shed (83C) with a Class 47 and Class 31 in residence. Note also the water crane and GWR semaphore signal with route indicator.

Below Turning slightly to the left from the previous picture, we see what would have been the shed yard, with Class 46 No 46028, Class 47 No 47094 and an unidentified Class 45 stabled. Part of what would have been the shed offices can be seen above the tank wagons. This picture, taken on 28 April 1984, also gives a better view of the water crane and interesting semaphore signal. Exeter shed closed to steam around 1964.

On 30 March 1991 a pair of Class 37s, Nos 37083 and 37230, together with Class 47 No 47200 and an HST unit were photographed outside the diesel depot at Bristol Bath Road. Part of the steam shed (see the picture on page 42 for comparison) can be seen to the left of the diesel depot. This MPD has now been closed.

THE STEAM LOCOMOTIVE SHED